AI INVESTMENT SECRETS

The Risks and Rewards of the Next Tech Revolution

How Artificial Intelligence is Shaping Financial Futures and What Investors Need to Know Now

Tom K. Smith

Copyright ©Tom K. Smith, 2024.

All rights reserved. No part of this publication may be reproduced, distributed, or transmitted in any form or by any means, including photocopying, recording, or other electronic or mechanical methods, without the prior written permission of the publisher, except in the case of brief quotations embodied in critical reviews and certain other noncommercial uses permitted by copyright law.

Table of Contents

Introduction..3
Chapter 1: Understanding AI Investments...............6
Chapter 2: The High-Growth Potential of AI............11
Chapter 3: Diverse Applications of AI......................21
Chapter 4: AI Investment Strategies: Stocks, Funds, and Venture Capital..32
Chapter 5: Market Volatility and the Challenges of AI Investing...44
Chapter 6: Regulatory and Ethical Challenges in AI... 56
Chapter 7: AI and Cybersecurity: The Need for Robust Protection... 70
Chapter 8: Separating Hype from Reality.................84
Chapter 9: AI Investment Opportunities in Startups... 99
Chapter 10: Long-Term AI Investment Strategies. 115
Chapter 11: The Future of AI.................................. 131
Conclusion... 149

Introduction

Artificial intelligence has moved from being a futuristic concept to a driving force in nearly every sector of modern technology. It is transforming industries, enabling breakthroughs in fields ranging from healthcare and finance to automotive and retail. At its core, AI has the ability to process massive amounts of data, recognize patterns, and make decisions with greater precision and efficiency than humans alone. This capability is reshaping how businesses operate and how people interact with technology, making AI one of the most significant technological shifts of our time.

For investors, AI represents an opportunity unlike any other. Companies at the forefront of AI development are seeing rapid growth as they continue to innovate and disrupt traditional industries. The promise of AI lies in its potential to revolutionize multiple sectors simultaneously, creating new business models, improving operational efficiencies, and opening up avenues for products and services that were once considered impossible. This creates immense potential for financial returns, especially for those who can recognize and invest in the right companies at the right time.

Yet, with this potential comes significant risk. The fast pace of AI development means that what is cutting-edge today could become obsolete tomorrow. Investors face the challenge of navigating a market that is not only evolving rapidly but is also subject to regulatory uncertainties and ethical concerns. These risks, combined with the volatility of tech stocks, make it essential for investors to understand both the opportunities and the challenges that come with AI investments.

In this book, we will explore the full spectrum of AI investments, delving into the immense opportunities it presents while also highlighting the risks that should not be overlooked. We will look at real-world examples of successful AI-driven companies, examine the various sectors AI is transforming, and discuss practical strategies for navigating this dynamic market. Whether you're a seasoned investor or someone new to the world of AI, this book will provide you with the insights you need to make informed decisions in a field that is reshaping the future of technology and business.

Chapter 1: Understanding AI Investments

Investing in artificial intelligence means allocating capital into technologies, companies, and services that are advancing AI's development and application. It involves backing the innovations that enable machines to perform tasks traditionally requiring human intelligence, such as learning from data, recognizing patterns, and making decisions. This can include investing in companies that are directly involved in creating AI technologies or in businesses that utilize AI to enhance their products and services.

To invest in AI is to tap into a field that is not only transforming industries but also shaping the future of global markets. Investors in AI aim to benefit financially from the rapid advancements in automation, machine learning, natural language processing, robotics, and other AI-related technologies. As AI continues to revolutionize sectors like healthcare, finance, transportation, and more, those who invest early in the right companies or technologies have the potential to see significant returns. However, these investments also come with risks, as the technology is still evolving, and the landscape can be unpredictable.

There are several categories of AI investment, each offering unique opportunities for investors to capitalize on the technology's growth and influence. One of the primary categories is direct investment in AI companies, which focuses on businesses that are at the forefront of AI development. These companies are typically engaged in creating algorithms, machine learning models, and AI-driven innovations that power various industries. Giants like Nvidia, with its leadership in creating GPUs essential for AI computation, or Alphabet, which has embedded AI in its products and services, are examples of companies driving AI forward.

Beyond direct company investments, there is also the realm of AI-driven software. This category includes companies that specialize in developing the algorithms and applications that enable machines to learn and perform complex tasks. These could be applications used for everything from customer service chatbots to predictive analytics in healthcare. As businesses across industries adopt AI-driven software, the demand for these solutions continues to grow, making this an attractive area for investors.

The third category is hardware, which underpins the AI revolution. Advanced computing power is required to run AI models and process large datasets at incredible speeds. Hardware companies that produce the specialized components, such as high-performance processors and chipsets, are critical in making AI possible. Investing in companies that manufacture or develop hardware specifically designed for AI provides a unique opportunity to be part of the technology's infrastructure.

Finally, there are AI services. As AI becomes more integrated into business operations, many companies seek external expertise to incorporate AI into their strategies without building in-house capabilities. AI-as-a-service providers offer cloud-based platforms that allow businesses to utilize AI tools without needing to invest in their own infrastructure. This category is growing rapidly, as more businesses seek to benefit from AI without the need for substantial upfront investment.

Across all of these categories, AI is impacting a wide range of industries, each with its own potential for transformation and growth. In healthcare, AI is being used to improve diagnostics, predict disease outbreaks, and even assist in the discovery of new drugs. It's not just enhancing operations, but changing how healthcare professionals interact with patients and approach treatment.

The finance industry has also been profoundly affected by AI, particularly through the use of algorithms for fraud detection, risk management, and trading. AI can analyze massive amounts of financial data in real-time, enabling more accurate predictions and more efficient decision-making processes.

In the automotive industry, AI is powering innovations such as autonomous vehicles, which are set to revolutionize transportation. Companies are using AI not only to develop self-driving cars but also to improve manufacturing processes, optimize logistics, and enhance safety features.

Other sectors, like retail, agriculture, and manufacturing, are seeing AI-driven innovations that increase efficiency, reduce costs, and create new business models. From personalized shopping experiences powered by recommendation engines to AI-powered robotics in agriculture that reduce waste, AI is transforming the way industries operate, presenting investors with numerous opportunities to engage in a wide range of markets.

Chapter 2: The High-Growth Potential of AI

Artificial intelligence is at the heart of innovation in today's most dynamic industries, transforming how businesses operate and create value. AI's ability to analyze vast amounts of data, recognize patterns, and automate complex tasks is unlocking new levels of efficiency, enabling faster decision-making, and creating entirely new products and services. This transformative power is being felt across a wide range of sectors, with AI-driven technologies fueling innovations that were unimaginable just a few years ago.

In healthcare, AI is changing the way doctors diagnose and treat diseases. Machine learning algorithms can now analyze medical images with incredible precision, detecting patterns that might be missed by human eyes. This leads to earlier diagnoses, improved treatment plans, and better patient outcomes. AI is also playing a crucial role in drug discovery, where it speeds up the process of identifying new compounds that could lead to life-saving medications. These advancements are not only improving healthcare but also making it more accessible and efficient.

The finance sector is also undergoing a significant transformation thanks to AI. Algorithms are being used to detect fraudulent transactions in real time, identify market trends, and optimize investment portfolios. AI's ability to process large datasets quickly and accurately gives financial institutions a competitive edge, enabling them to offer more personalized services and make better decisions. High-frequency trading, powered by AI algorithms that execute trades at lightning speed, is another example of how AI is reshaping finance.

In the automotive industry, AI is driving the development of autonomous vehicles. Companies like Tesla have pioneered the use of AI to create self-driving technology, revolutionizing transportation and logistics. AI not only powers the vehicles themselves but also enhances the efficiency of manufacturing processes, enabling companies to produce vehicles more quickly and at lower costs. As self-driving technology continues to advance, the potential for disruption in the automotive industry is immense, with new business models emerging around ride-sharing and logistics automation.

Retailers are also leveraging AI to enhance the shopping experience. Recommendation engines powered by AI analyze customer behavior to suggest products that consumers are most likely to buy, personalizing the shopping experience in a way that boosts sales. AI is also being used to optimize inventory management, ensuring that products are available when and where they are needed. In e-commerce, AI-powered chatbots and customer service tools allow businesses to provide 24/7 assistance to customers, improving satisfaction and driving repeat business.

Manufacturing and agriculture are seeing AI-driven innovations that are improving productivity and reducing costs. In manufacturing, AI-powered robots can work alongside humans, performing repetitive tasks with precision and speed. These robots are not only increasing output but also reducing the risk of workplace injuries. In agriculture, AI is being used to monitor crop health, optimize irrigation, and reduce the use of pesticides, helping farmers improve yields while minimizing environmental impact.

At the forefront of these innovations are high-growth companies that are leading the charge in AI development. Companies like Nvidia, Alphabet, Microsoft, and Amazon are all investing heavily in AI, creating technologies that are pushing the boundaries of what's possible. Nvidia's advanced GPUs are essential for AI computation, enabling the processing of the vast datasets needed for machine learning models. Alphabet is integrating AI into its core services, from search algorithms to cloud computing solutions, making AI accessible to businesses of all sizes. Microsoft is investing in AI-powered tools that enhance productivity, from AI-driven analytics in Office applications to its Azure AI cloud platform. Amazon, with its AI-powered recommendation engine and logistics systems, continues to set the standard for how AI can be used to enhance customer experiences and streamline operations.

These companies are not only developing cutting-edge technologies but are also playing a critical role in shaping the future of AI. Their innovations are setting the pace for the industry, with other companies and startups following their lead. As AI continues to evolve, these high-growth firms are likely to remain at the forefront, driving further advancements and opening new opportunities for investors and businesses alike.

Tesla and Amazon provide two of the most compelling examples of how artificial intelligence is driving not only technological innovation but also significant business growth. Tesla, under the leadership of Elon Musk, has positioned itself as a pioneer in the automotive industry by embedding

AI into the core of its mission. One of the company's most notable achievements is its development of autonomous driving technologies, which rely on AI-powered systems to navigate roads, detect obstacles, and make real-time decisions. Tesla's Autopilot and Full Self-Driving (FSD) systems are constantly improving through machine learning algorithms that gather data from millions of miles driven by Tesla vehicles. This AI-driven approach has allowed Tesla to not only stay ahead in the race for self-driving cars but also create a platform for future advancements in transportation.

Tesla's use of AI goes beyond just autonomous driving. The company is utilizing AI in its manufacturing processes, optimizing production lines and reducing waste, which ultimately improves efficiency and lowers costs. Tesla's long-term strategy is also built on the idea that AI will continue to play a pivotal role in the future of energy, particularly with AI-driven energy storage solutions that will complement its electric vehicle ecosystem. Tesla's stock has reflected the market's confidence in its AI-driven innovation, showing massive growth over the years, largely due to its technological leadership in the automotive space.

Amazon, on the other hand, has revolutionized the retail and logistics industries by integrating AI into nearly every facet of its business. The company's recommendation engine, one of the most well-known uses of AI, has transformed the online shopping experience by analyzing user behavior to suggest products that customers are more likely to buy. This personalization not only improves customer satisfaction but also drives sales and increases customer loyalty. Behind the scenes, AI is powering Amazon's massive logistics network, optimizing supply chains and ensuring that products are delivered to customers as quickly and efficiently as possible. The use of AI-powered robots in Amazon's fulfillment centers is another example of how the company is leveraging AI to stay ahead of the competition.

Beyond e-commerce, Amazon's AI influence is expanding through its cloud computing division, Amazon Web Services (AWS). AWS offers AI-as-a-service, providing businesses with access to powerful machine learning tools and AI-driven services without the need for significant upfront investment. This democratization of AI has allowed countless businesses to integrate AI into their operations, further enhancing Amazon's position as a leader in AI innovation.

Looking toward the future, trends such as autonomous vehicles and smart cities are set to shape the AI investment landscape in profound ways. Autonomous vehicles, like those being developed by Tesla and other automotive giants, represent a massive shift in transportation. These vehicles will rely heavily on AI to navigate, communicate with other vehicles, and make decisions on the road, all without human intervention. The market for autonomous vehicles is projected to grow exponentially as AI technology matures, and companies that are leading the charge in this space could see significant financial gains. Investors who position themselves early in these developments stand to benefit from the growing demand for autonomous driving solutions, not just in passenger vehicles but also in logistics and delivery services.

Smart cities are another trend that will heavily influence AI investments in the coming years. These cities will integrate AI into their infrastructure to manage traffic, optimize energy use, and improve public services. AI systems in smart cities could control everything from streetlights that adjust based on real-time traffic data to waste management systems that predict and plan for pickup routes. As urbanization continues and cities look for ways to become more efficient and sustainable, the demand for AI-driven solutions will rise, presenting a lucrative opportunity for AI-focused companies and investors.

The future of AI investments is vast, with opportunities ranging from advancements in transportation to innovations in urban infrastructure. Companies that are able to harness the power of AI in these areas are poised for significant growth, and investors who recognize these trends early will have the chance to capitalize on AI's transformative impact across various industries. Whether it's the race for autonomous vehicles or the evolution of smart cities, AI will continue to drive the next wave of technological advancements, reshaping industries and economies worldwide.

Chapter 3: Diverse Applications of AI

Artificial intelligence is making profound inroads into a variety of industries, with its applications in healthcare, finance, transportation, and manufacturing leading to dramatic improvements in both operational efficiency and customer satisfaction. Each of these sectors is leveraging AI in unique ways, fundamentally changing how businesses and services operate.

In healthcare, AI has become a transformative force, particularly in diagnostics and treatment planning. Machine learning algorithms are being used to analyze medical images and detect diseases such as cancer with a level of accuracy that was once impossible. These AI-driven systems can process and interpret data far faster than humans, leading to quicker diagnoses and enabling healthcare providers to make informed decisions more efficiently. AI is also being employed in drug discovery, where it helps researchers identify new potential compounds, drastically reducing the time and cost associated with bringing new treatments to market. Moreover, AI-powered chatbots and virtual health assistants are improving patient engagement, providing round-the-clock support, and answering medical queries, thus increasing patient satisfaction and reducing the burden on healthcare professionals.

The finance industry has also embraced AI, using it to streamline operations and enhance customer service. One of the most impactful uses of AI in finance is in fraud detection, where AI systems continuously monitor transactions in real time, identifying suspicious activity and reducing the risk of fraud. Additionally, AI algorithms are used in risk assessment and credit scoring, allowing financial institutions to make faster, more accurate lending decisions. AI is also powering the rise of algorithmic trading, where systems analyze market data at incredible speeds, making split-second trading decisions that human traders could never achieve. This automation is driving efficiency in financial markets while allowing institutions to offer personalized financial advice to their clients, tailored to their spending habits, saving patterns, and investment goals.

In transportation, AI is revolutionizing how goods and people move. Self-driving technology is the most prominent example, with companies like Tesla leading the way in developing autonomous vehicles that can navigate roads, avoid obstacles, and adapt to changing driving conditions without human intervention. AI systems are also improving route optimization for logistics and delivery services, allowing companies to save time and fuel while improving delivery times. AI-powered traffic management systems are being implemented in smart cities, analyzing real-time traffic data to reduce congestion, optimize traffic lights, and improve overall urban mobility. For airlines, AI is helping in predictive maintenance, analyzing sensor data from aircraft to anticipate mechanical issues before they cause delays or safety risks, thus improving operational reliability and passenger satisfaction.

In manufacturing, AI is driving the automation of production lines and improving the precision of industrial processes. AI-powered robots are now working alongside humans in factories, handling repetitive tasks with greater speed and accuracy, reducing errors, and increasing output. These robots can also adapt to new tasks through machine learning, which makes them highly versatile for different stages of production. Predictive maintenance is another area where AI is having a significant impact. By analyzing data from sensors on equipment, AI systems can predict when a machine is likely to fail and schedule maintenance before a breakdown occurs, minimizing downtime and keeping production running smoothly. AI is also being used in quality control, where machine learning algorithms inspect products on the assembly line to detect defects faster and more reliably than the human eye. This helps manufacturers maintain high standards of quality, reduce waste, and ensure that customer satisfaction remains high.

In all of these sectors, AI is more than just a tool for automation—it is enabling businesses to operate more efficiently and make smarter decisions. By processing vast amounts of data, identifying trends, and predicting outcomes, AI is helping companies optimize their operations while simultaneously improving the customer experience. Whether it's by enabling faster diagnoses in healthcare, reducing financial fraud, optimizing logistics in transportation, or increasing productivity in manufacturing, AI is delivering tangible benefits that are reshaping entire industries.

Several companies across industries have successfully integrated artificial intelligence into their operations, disrupting traditional business models and achieving significant growth. These companies have harnessed the power of AI to streamline operations, enhance customer experience, and innovate in ways that set them apart from competitors. Here are a few notable case studies that highlight how AI has been a game-changer for businesses:

One of the most compelling examples is **Tesla**, which has leveraged AI to revolutionize the automotive industry. Tesla's use of AI is most evident in its development of autonomous driving technology. The company's Autopilot and Full Self-Driving (FSD) systems rely on AI to navigate roads, detect obstacles, and make real-time decisions based on millions of data points collected from Tesla vehicles worldwide. This data-driven approach has allowed Tesla to improve the performance of its self-driving technology through machine learning, positioning the company as a leader in the race toward fully autonomous vehicles. Additionally, Tesla uses AI to optimize its manufacturing processes, improving efficiency and lowering costs, which has contributed to its rapid growth and market dominance in electric vehicles.

Tesla's AI-driven approach to both technology and production has set it apart in an industry traditionally resistant to change.

Amazon is another prime example of a company that has successfully integrated AI to disrupt multiple industries, particularly in retail and logistics. Amazon's recommendation engine, powered by AI, analyzes customer behavior to suggest products that users are likely to buy, increasing the likelihood of sales and improving the overall shopping experience. This personalization, which is driven by AI algorithms that constantly learn from user interactions, has been a key factor in Amazon's e-commerce success. In logistics, Amazon uses AI to optimize its vast network of warehouses and delivery routes. AI-powered robots now handle many tasks in Amazon's fulfillment centers, speeding up the processing and shipping of orders while reducing costs. Furthermore, Amazon Web Services (AWS) offers AI-as-a-service, allowing businesses to use Amazon's AI tools and infrastructure to enhance their own operations. This integration of AI across its services has helped Amazon maintain its leadership in e-commerce and cloud computing, making it one of the most valuable companies in the world.

Another notable example is **Netflix**, which has transformed the entertainment industry through its use of AI. Netflix's recommendation system is central to its business model, using AI to analyze user preferences and viewing habits to suggest content that subscribers are likely to enjoy. This personalized approach keeps viewers engaged, reduces churn, and increases customer satisfaction, which in turn boosts subscription growth. Netflix also uses AI to optimize its content production decisions, analyzing data to determine what types of shows and movies will perform well with different audience segments. This data-driven approach has allowed Netflix to create hit shows and films that cater to specific tastes, further increasing its global appeal and competitive edge in the streaming market.

In the financial sector, **JP Morgan Chase** has integrated AI into its operations to disrupt traditional banking and enhance customer experience. The company uses AI for fraud detection, analyzing transaction data in real time to identify suspicious activity and protect customers. AI also powers the bank's customer service chatbot, which helps customers manage their accounts, make payments, and receive personalized financial advice. Additionally, JP Morgan has adopted AI for algorithmic trading, using machine learning models to analyze market data and execute trades with speed and precision. This integration of AI has allowed the bank to improve efficiency, reduce costs, and provide better services to its clients.

In the realm of agriculture, **Blue River Technology**, acquired by John Deere, has developed AI-powered solutions that are transforming farming practices. Their flagship product, See & Spray, uses computer vision and machine learning to identify weeds in real-time and spray herbicide only where it's needed. This precision agriculture approach significantly reduces the amount of herbicide used, lowering costs for farmers while promoting more sustainable farming practices. The success of Blue River Technology's AI solutions has had a profound impact on the agricultural industry, helping farmers increase yields and reduce environmental impact.

These case studies demonstrate the power of AI to disrupt industries by improving operational efficiency, enhancing customer satisfaction, and driving innovation. Companies that have successfully integrated AI into their business models are not only gaining a competitive edge but are also setting the stage for long-term growth. Whether in automotive, retail, entertainment, finance, or agriculture, AI is proving to be a transformative force that enables businesses to reimagine what's possible in their respective industries.

Chapter 4: AI Investment Strategies: Stocks, Funds, and Venture Capital

When it comes to investing in artificial intelligence, there are several pathways available to investors, each offering distinct advantages and challenges. Depending on the investor's goals, risk tolerance, and level of involvement, options like direct stock purchases, mutual funds, ETFs, and venture capital provide diverse opportunities to gain exposure to the rapidly growing AI sector. Understanding the pros and cons of each strategy is crucial for making informed investment decisions.

One of the most direct ways to invest in AI is by purchasing **individual stocks** of companies that are at the forefront of AI development. Companies like Nvidia, Alphabet (Google), Microsoft, and Amazon are some of the biggest players in the AI space. By investing in these stocks, an investor can directly benefit from the growth of these companies as they continue to innovate and integrate AI into their operations. The key advantage of this approach is the potential for high returns, especially if the investor selects companies that experience significant growth due to their AI-driven innovations. However, this strategy also carries a high level of risk, particularly because tech stocks can be volatile. The rapid pace of AI development means that what is considered cutting-edge today may quickly become outdated, leading to fluctuations in stock prices. Furthermore, choosing the right AI companies requires in-depth research and a solid understanding of the market, as not all companies will succeed in capitalizing on AI.

For investors seeking a more diversified approach, **mutual funds** and **ETFs (exchange-traded funds)** that focus on AI and technology sectors offer a less risky alternative. These funds pool money from many investors and invest in a broad range of companies involved in AI, thus spreading the risk across multiple stocks. One of the main advantages of mutual funds and ETFs is diversification. By investing in a variety of

AI-focused companies, investors reduce the risk of losing money due to the poor performance of any single stock. ETFs, in particular, offer the additional benefit of being more liquid than mutual funds, as they can be traded like individual stocks on exchanges. However, while the risk is lower compared to individual stocks, so is the potential for high returns, as gains are spread out over multiple companies rather than concentrated in one. Moreover, these funds often come with management fees, which can eat into the investor's profits over time.

Venture capital (VC), on the other hand, represents a high-risk, high-reward strategy for investors with a greater appetite for risk. Venture capital involves investing in early-stage startups that are developing cutting-edge AI technologies. The appeal of this approach lies in the potential for outsized returns. If a startup backed by venture capital succeeds in creating breakthrough AI technology, the rewards for early investors can be enormous. For example, many venture capitalists who invested early in companies like Tesla or Google reaped substantial gains as these companies grew into global giants. However, the downside is that venture capital is extremely risky. Many startups fail to take off, and investors may lose their entire investment if the company does not succeed. Additionally, venture capital investments are typically illiquid, meaning that investors may have to wait several years to see any returns, if at all.

In addition to these pathways, there are also **AI-focused mutual funds** that specialize in investing in companies across various sectors that are heavily involved in AI development and implementation. These funds offer a balance between diversification and targeted exposure to AI-related businesses. They can provide a way for investors to gain access to AI investments without having to pick individual stocks, while still benefiting from the growth potential in this space. However, mutual funds typically come with higher management fees than ETFs, and investors do not have as much control over the specific companies included in the fund.

Each of these strategies—whether it be direct stocks, mutual funds, ETFs, or venture capital—offers unique benefits and trade-offs. **Direct stock investing** provides the potential for high returns but comes with significant volatility and the need for careful stock selection. **Mutual funds and ETFs** offer diversification and lower risk but may result in more moderate returns. **Venture capital** presents the chance for large rewards but carries the highest level of risk and often requires a long-term commitment. Investors need to carefully consider their risk tolerance, financial goals, and level of market knowledge before deciding on the best approach to AI investment.

Ultimately, a successful AI investment strategy may involve a combination of these approaches, allowing investors to balance risk and reward while gaining exposure to one of the most transformative technologies of our time.

Diversifying an AI investment portfolio is essential for achieving a balance between potential high returns and minimizing risk. Artificial intelligence, as a rapidly evolving technology, offers vast opportunities but comes with considerable uncertainties due to its constantly shifting landscape. Diversification involves spreading investments across various AI sectors, companies, and asset types to reduce the exposure to any single company or technology that may not succeed as expected.

To start, investors should consider **investing in different sectors** within AI. While AI itself is a distinct technology, it touches many industries, including healthcare, finance, automotive, and retail. By diversifying across these sectors, investors can mitigate the risk of sector-specific challenges. For example, the automotive industry may experience regulatory hurdles that slow down the adoption of autonomous vehicles, while healthcare AI could thrive due to the increasing demand for medical innovations. This sectoral diversification ensures that an investor's portfolio is not overly reliant on the success or failure of one particular application of AI.

Geographic diversification is another strategy for balancing risk. AI development is global, with major advancements taking place in regions such as North America, Europe, and Asia. Companies from these regions may face different regulatory environments, market conditions, and opportunities. By investing in AI companies from various geographic locations, an investor can take advantage of different growth drivers while buffering against regional market downturns or political challenges.

Investors should also consider a mix of **investment vehicles**—such as individual stocks, mutual funds, ETFs, and venture capital. For example, an investor might hold individual stocks in large, well-established AI companies for stability, while also investing in ETFs that track AI-focused indexes to gain exposure to a broader range of companies. Additionally, a small portion of the portfolio could be allocated to venture capital or funds focused on emerging AI startups to capture high-growth potential, albeit with higher risk. This approach balances the security provided by established companies with the possibility of outsized returns from innovative startups.

When building an AI investment portfolio, **some key companies** stand out due to their leadership and innovation in AI technology. **Nvidia** is one of the most important players in AI hardware, particularly with its development of advanced GPUs that are essential for training AI models. Nvidia's GPUs power many AI applications, from machine learning to gaming, making the company a crucial player in the AI ecosystem. Nvidia's growth prospects remain strong as AI technologies continue to evolve, requiring ever more powerful computational resources.

Alphabet (Google) is another critical company in the AI landscape. As the parent company of Google, Alphabet has made AI a core part of its business strategy, embedding machine learning in its search algorithms, advertising platforms, and Google Cloud services. Alphabet's DeepMind division is known for its groundbreaking work in AI research, including achievements like AlphaGo, the AI that defeated a world champion in the board game Go. Alphabet's vast data resources, combined with its expertise in AI, position the company to continue driving innovation in the field.

Microsoft is also a key player in AI, particularly through its cloud computing platform, Azure, which offers AI and machine learning services to businesses worldwide. Microsoft's AI tools and services are designed to help organizations of all sizes implement AI into their operations. Additionally, Microsoft's investment in OpenAI, the organization behind advanced language models like GPT, shows its commitment to staying at the forefront of AI development. Microsoft has integrated AI into its products, from Office applications to its customer relationship management software, making it a major force in the AI-driven transformation of business processes.

Alongside these tech giants, there are numerous **emerging AI startups** that are pushing the boundaries of AI innovation. Companies like **UiPath**, which specializes in robotic process automation (RPA), are using AI to automate routine business tasks, allowing organizations to improve efficiency and reduce costs. **Palantir**, known for its work in data analytics and AI-driven decision-making tools, has made significant strides in sectors such as defense, government, and healthcare. Another promising startup is **C3.ai**, which focuses on enterprise AI software, providing AI solutions to improve decision-making, optimize operations, and enhance customer engagement.

Investors should keep an eye on these emerging companies, as they often represent opportunities for high growth. While investing in startups carries more risk than established companies, the potential for significant returns is much higher, especially if a startup successfully disrupts an industry or introduces a transformative AI solution.

By diversifying across well-established giants like Nvidia, Alphabet, and Microsoft, while also including emerging startups, investors can build a portfolio that balances **stability with growth potential**. The larger companies provide a more secure investment, given their proven track record and resources, while the startups offer exposure to the next wave of AI innovations that could shape the future.

Ultimately, a diversified AI investment portfolio is one that not only captures the transformative potential of AI but also minimizes the risks associated with rapid technological changes. Whether through different sectors, geographies, or investment vehicles, balancing a portfolio allows investors to participate in the AI revolution while ensuring long-term stability.

Chapter 5: Market Volatility and the Challenges of AI Investing

The artificial intelligence sector, while full of promise, is also inherently volatile due to the rapid pace of technological change. For investors, this volatility poses both significant opportunities and risks. AI companies are often at the forefront of cutting-edge innovation, and breakthroughs in AI can lead to surges in stock prices as investors scramble to capitalize on new advancements. However, the speed at which technology evolves also means that what is considered groundbreaking today may quickly become outdated, putting pressure on AI companies to continuously innovate or risk falling behind.

One of the primary reasons for market volatility in AI is the continuous development of new AI models, algorithms, and applications. These advances can significantly disrupt industries, shifting market dynamics and driving the stock prices of companies either upward or downward, depending on how well they keep up with the latest trends. For example, when a company announces a major breakthrough in AI, such as a new machine learning algorithm or an innovative AI-powered product, the market typically responds positively, leading to a sharp rise in that company's stock price. However, this enthusiasm can quickly wane if competitors introduce superior technology, or if the innovation doesn't translate into immediate commercial success.

Moreover, AI companies often operate in an environment of high expectations. Investors are keenly aware of the enormous potential that AI holds, and as a result, they frequently price in future growth when evaluating AI stocks. This speculative nature of AI investments can lead to significant volatility, as stock prices can swing dramatically based on the perceived progress (or lack thereof) that companies make in AI development. In addition, regulatory changes, competition, and ethical concerns can contribute to fluctuations in stock prices, making the AI sector highly sensitive to external factors.

Another critical risk that investors must consider is **technological obsolescence**. In the AI field, innovations happen at a breakneck pace, and companies that fail to keep up may find their products or services becoming obsolete almost overnight. AI technologies, particularly in areas like machine learning, natural language processing, and robotics, are continuously being refined and improved. For example, a company that creates a popular AI tool or platform today may find that a competitor introduces a more efficient or effective solution tomorrow, rendering the original product outdated and less valuable. This rapid cycle of innovation can create significant challenges for AI companies trying to maintain their competitive edge.

Technological obsolescence not only affects AI-driven products and services but also the hardware and infrastructure that support AI operations. AI systems require vast computing power, and advancements in hardware, such as new processors or GPUs, can quickly render older technologies inefficient or uncompetitive. Companies that rely on outdated hardware may struggle to keep up with the performance and scalability demands of modern AI applications, leading to a loss of market share and declining stock prices.

In addition to hardware, AI software platforms also face obsolescence risks. New algorithms or techniques that significantly improve performance or accuracy can make existing AI models outdated. For example, an AI company that develops a successful image recognition tool may see its product lose value if a competitor introduces a new model that can perform the same tasks with greater speed or accuracy. Investors in AI must be aware of these risks and understand that a company's ability to innovate and stay ahead of the curve is crucial for maintaining its market position.

This constant need for innovation also puts pressure on AI companies to invest heavily in research and development. While this can drive significant breakthroughs, it can also strain resources and lead to financial instability if new innovations fail to produce the expected returns. Smaller companies, in particular, may struggle to compete with larger, more established firms that have greater resources to invest in long-term AI research. This creates a situation where even promising startups can quickly fall behind if they are unable to keep pace with technological advancements.

For investors, the rapid pace of change in AI technology means that they must stay informed and closely monitor the companies in which they invest. It's important to look for AI companies that demonstrate a strong commitment to innovation, have a proven track record of adapting to new technologies, and have the financial stability to weather periods of volatility. Companies that can successfully navigate the challenges of technological obsolescence are more likely to emerge as leaders in the AI space, offering long-term growth potential.

In summary, market volatility in AI is largely driven by the rapid pace of technological change, with stock prices reacting swiftly to both breakthroughs and setbacks. The risk of technological obsolescence adds another layer of complexity, as AI technologies can become outdated quickly if companies fail to innovate. For investors, understanding these dynamics is key to making informed decisions and managing the risks associated with AI investments. While the potential rewards are significant, the fast-moving nature of the industry requires careful attention to ensure that investments are aligned with companies capable of sustaining long-term growth in a highly competitive environment.

Balancing risk and reward is at the heart of any investment strategy, and this principle is especially critical when it comes to artificial intelligence. The AI sector, though brimming with opportunities for explosive growth, is also marked by inherent volatility and uncertainty. For investors looking to navigate this dynamic and fast-paced landscape, adopting a long-term perspective is essential.

One of the key reasons a long-term view is crucial for AI investment is the **slow maturation of AI technologies**. While AI is transforming industries and creating new opportunities, many of the most significant advancements in AI—such as fully autonomous vehicles, advanced robotics, or AI-powered healthcare diagnostics—are still in the development stage. It may take years, or even decades, for these innovations to reach their full potential and become widespread. As a result, short-term investors may not see immediate returns from their AI investments, leading to frustration or hasty decisions to exit the market. Those who take a longer view, however, are better positioned to benefit from the eventual maturation of these technologies, as companies that lead AI innovations are likely to see their stock prices soar as their breakthroughs become mainstream.

Another reason why a long-term perspective is vital is the **volatility that characterizes the AI industry**. As discussed earlier, AI companies are often subject to sharp price swings due to the rapid pace of technological change, investor sentiment, and market competition. In the short term, this volatility can be unsettling, as stocks may experience significant declines based on temporary setbacks, regulatory issues, or competition. However, those who adopt a long-term outlook understand that the AI sector is still in its early stages and that short-term fluctuations are a natural part of its growth. Over time, as AI continues to advance and prove its value across various industries, the market is likely to reward those companies that are leading innovation and creating sustainable business models.

Furthermore, AI investment demands patience because **the path to profitability can be slow**.

Many AI companies, particularly startups, invest heavily in research and development (R&D) to stay at the cutting edge of innovation. While this R&D spending is critical to their long-term success, it can delay profitability, especially in the early stages of a company's growth. Investors who focus solely on short-term profits may miss out on substantial long-term gains by pulling out too early. However, those with a longer perspective can ride out periods of heavy R&D spending, understanding that these investments are essential for the company to capture future growth in the AI market.

The nature of AI as a **disruptive technology** also reinforces the importance of a long-term approach. AI is reshaping industries such as healthcare, finance, transportation, and retail, but this disruption takes time. Incumbent companies may resist change, regulatory frameworks may lag behind technological advancements, and consumers may be slow to adopt new AI-driven products and services. Investors who recognize that

AI's full impact may unfold gradually over many years will be better positioned to reap the rewards of long-term disruption. As AI continues to integrate into daily life and revolutionize industries, the companies that are at the forefront of this transformation will see significant long-term value creation, making early investments in these companies potentially highly rewarding.

Moreover, taking a long-term perspective allows investors to focus on **quality and sustainability** rather than short-term hype. The AI space is often filled with excitement about the latest breakthroughs, leading to speculative bubbles around new technologies or companies. By thinking long term, investors can evaluate whether a company has a sustainable competitive advantage, robust leadership, and a solid business model capable of delivering consistent value. This reduces the temptation to chase short-term gains from overhyped technologies that may not stand the test of time.

Investors who adopt a long-term strategy also benefit from **compounding growth**. As AI technologies become more embedded in various industries, companies that innovate in AI are likely to experience exponential growth. The compounding effect of sustained earnings, reinvestment in innovation, and expanding market reach can lead to significant returns over time. While short-term investors may be discouraged by the inevitable setbacks along the way, long-term investors are positioned to benefit from this cumulative growth.

In summary, the AI industry's rapid evolution, volatility, and the long runway required for many of its most transformative technologies to fully mature make a long-term perspective essential for investors. By focusing on the bigger picture, remaining patient, and understanding that AI will continue to shape the future of industries worldwide, investors can balance the risks and rewards effectively. The long-term outlook enables investors to weather short-term volatility, avoid being swayed by momentary setbacks, and ultimately capitalize on the profound changes that AI will bring to the global economy.

Chapter 6: Regulatory and Ethical Challenges in AI

The current state of AI regulation is still in its infancy, as governments around the world struggle to keep pace with the rapid development and deployment of artificial intelligence technologies. AI's transformative potential across industries has created an urgent need for regulatory frameworks that can ensure these technologies are used ethically, safely, and in ways that protect the public. However, due to the complexity of AI and its wide range of applications, governments are finding it challenging to establish clear, comprehensive policies that address both the opportunities and risks associated with AI.

One of the main challenges for regulators is the **broad scope of AI technologies** and their varied uses. From healthcare diagnostics to autonomous vehicles, AI systems are employed in numerous fields, each with its own set of regulatory needs. In some areas, like transportation, existing laws can be adapted to cover new technologies like self-driving cars. However, in other sectors, such as healthcare or finance, AI is introducing entirely new ways of working that require regulators to craft rules from the ground up. This process is slow and often lags behind technological innovation, creating a regulatory gap where AI can advance without proper oversight.

Additionally, many governments are cautious about over-regulating AI for fear of stifling innovation. AI is seen as a critical driver of future economic growth, and countries are eager to establish themselves as leaders in the AI race. Overly stringent regulations could limit experimentation and slow the development of new AI technologies, putting certain regions at a competitive disadvantage. As a result, governments are walking a fine line between creating rules that protect the public and allowing enough flexibility for innovation to thrive.

In response to these challenges, some countries have adopted **guiding principles** for AI regulation rather than prescriptive rules. For example, the European Union's General Data Protection Regulation (GDPR) includes provisions related to AI, such as the right to explanation, which requires AI systems to explain their decisions when they significantly impact individuals. The EU has also proposed the AI Act, which seeks to create a risk-based framework for regulating AI applications, categorizing them by the level of risk they pose. High-risk AI systems, like those used in critical infrastructure or law enforcement, would be subject to stricter oversight, while low-risk systems would face fewer restrictions. In the United States, regulation is more fragmented, with different agencies overseeing specific sectors. However, the government has recently begun exploring broader AI policies, including the National AI Initiative, which aims to coordinate AI research and development across federal agencies.

As governments grapple with regulating AI, **ethical concerns** have become a central focus. One of the most pressing issues is **data privacy**. AI systems often rely on vast amounts of personal data to function effectively, whether it's through analyzing medical records, financial transactions, or online behavior. This reliance on data raises significant privacy concerns, as individuals may not fully understand how their data is being used or stored. In cases where data is mishandled or exposed to security breaches, public trust in AI technologies can be severely damaged. Governments are working to create regulations that protect personal data while allowing AI systems to function effectively, but striking this balance remains a challenge.

Another ethical concern is **algorithmic bias**, which can occur when AI systems inadvertently reflect or amplify societal biases present in the data they are trained on. For example, an AI system used for hiring might be biased against certain demographic groups if the historical data it was trained on reflects unequal hiring practices. Similarly, facial recognition technologies have been shown to perform less accurately for people of color, leading to potential discrimination. These biases can have serious real-world consequences, from unfair hiring decisions to wrongful arrests, and they raise important questions about the fairness and accountability of AI systems. Governments and AI developers are increasingly focused on creating frameworks to ensure that AI systems are trained on unbiased data and that their decisions are transparent and explainable.

The impact of these ethical concerns on **public perception** of AI cannot be overstated. While AI holds great promise, the potential for harm—whether through privacy violations or biased decision-making—has made many people wary of the technology. Public trust in AI is critical for its widespread adoption, particularly in sensitive areas like healthcare, law enforcement, and finance. If people believe that AI systems are unfair or that their personal data is not being adequately protected, they are less likely to support the use of AI in these areas. To address this, governments and companies alike are working to improve transparency around AI technologies, ensuring that the public understands how AI systems work, how decisions are made, and what steps are being taken to protect privacy and prevent bias.

In response to these ethical concerns, some tech companies have adopted **self-regulatory practices**, developing internal guidelines to ensure their AI technologies are used responsibly. Many companies now conduct regular audits of their AI systems to check for biases, improve transparency, and ensure compliance with emerging regulations. However, self-regulation is not a long-term solution, and many experts agree that government oversight is essential to ensure that AI is developed and deployed in ways that serve the public interest.

In conclusion, AI regulation is still evolving, and governments are facing significant challenges in keeping up with the rapid pace of technological change. Ethical concerns around data privacy and algorithmic bias are shaping the conversation, as both regulators and the public push for greater transparency and fairness in AI systems. While the current state of regulation remains fragmented and inconsistent, the efforts to create more robust frameworks for AI oversight are gaining momentum. As AI continues to reshape industries and everyday life, the balance between innovation, regulation, and ethics will be crucial in determining how these technologies are integrated into society.

The challenges surrounding AI regulation, ethical concerns, and public perception can have profound effects on the valuations of AI companies and the overall stability of the AI market. As governments and regulators grapple with establishing frameworks to manage AI's impact, and as ethical issues such as data privacy and algorithmic bias remain front and center, companies in the AI sector face increased scrutiny. This, in turn, can lead to market fluctuations and shifts in investor confidence.

One of the primary ways that regulatory challenges impact AI company valuations is through **uncertainty**. The lack of clear and consistent regulatory frameworks for AI creates a degree of unpredictability that makes it difficult for investors to assess the long-term growth potential of AI companies. For example, if a government were to suddenly impose stringent regulations on the use of AI in certain industries, companies that rely heavily on these technologies could face significant operational costs to ensure compliance. This regulatory burden can slow down innovation, delay product launches, and increase the cost of doing business, which can negatively impact stock prices and company valuations.

Additionally, uncertainty about **future regulation** may cause investors to hesitate in backing AI companies, particularly startups that are still in the development stage. If investors are unsure how AI technologies will be regulated in the future, they may perceive these companies as too risky, leading to lower investment and, subsequently, lower valuations. Even large, well-established AI companies like Alphabet or Microsoft are not immune to this uncertainty. If these companies are required to alter their AI-driven services or products to comply with new regulations, it could affect their profitability and growth prospects.

Another significant factor affecting AI company valuations is the **public perception of ethical issues**, particularly data privacy and algorithmic bias. Companies that are perceived as mishandling user data or engaging in unethical AI practices may face public backlash, which can severely damage their reputation and brand. This erosion of public trust can have a direct impact on a company's customer base, reducing demand for its products and services. In an era where consumers are becoming increasingly aware of how their data is used, AI companies must be transparent and proactive in addressing privacy concerns, or they risk losing both customers and investor confidence.

The issue of **algorithmic bias** further complicates the landscape for AI companies. If an AI system is found to be biased—whether in hiring, lending, or law enforcement—it can lead to lawsuits, regulatory fines, or government intervention, all of which can significantly hurt a company's financial standing. For example, if a company's AI-driven hiring platform is found to discriminate against certain demographic groups, it could not only face legal consequences but also lose the trust of clients who rely on its technology for recruitment. Negative publicity from such incidents can cause stock prices to drop and can lead to investors questioning the company's ability to effectively manage and deploy AI technologies.

In extreme cases, widespread **ethical violations** or data breaches involving AI can destabilize the market as a whole. If a leading AI company experiences a major scandal, it can trigger broader investor concerns about the entire AI sector. For instance, a large-scale privacy breach involving an AI-driven platform could result in regulatory crackdowns that affect multiple companies across the industry, leading to volatility in AI-related stocks. Similarly, if governments begin to introduce regulations in response to public concerns about AI's impact on jobs, privacy, or security, it could create additional compliance costs for AI companies and negatively impact market stability.

Litigation and legal liabilities are another way in which these challenges affect AI valuations. As AI technologies continue to advance, there is growing legal ambiguity around issues such as accountability for AI-driven decisions. Who is responsible when an AI-powered autonomous vehicle is involved in an accident? What legal recourse do individuals have if an AI system denies them a loan or a job based on biased data? These unresolved legal questions add to the complexity of operating in the AI space and can increase the likelihood of expensive lawsuits. For investors, this legal uncertainty introduces additional risk, which can result in lower valuations for companies that rely heavily on AI technologies.

Moreover, **investor confidence** can be shaken by the perception that AI companies are not doing enough to address ethical concerns. In the current business climate, where environmental, social, and governance (ESG) criteria are becoming increasingly important, investors are paying close attention to how companies handle issues like privacy, fairness, and accountability in AI. Companies that fail to prioritize ethical AI development may find it difficult to attract institutional investors or venture capital, which can negatively impact their valuations and growth potential.

On the flip side, companies that proactively engage with regulators and prioritize ethical AI development stand to benefit from increased investor confidence. By demonstrating a commitment to responsible AI practices and transparent data handling, these companies can position themselves as leaders in a market that is becoming increasingly scrutinized. In fact, AI companies that successfully navigate these regulatory and ethical challenges are likely to see their valuations rise, as investors will view them as more stable, reliable, and forward-thinking.

In conclusion, the regulatory and ethical challenges surrounding AI can have a significant impact on company valuations and market stability. Uncertainty about future regulations, public concerns over data privacy and algorithmic bias, and the potential for legal liabilities all contribute to the risks that AI companies face. However, companies that take proactive steps to address these challenges and build trust with consumers and regulators can position themselves for long-term success, potentially emerging as leaders in an increasingly complex and regulated market. Investors, in turn, must carefully assess how AI companies are managing these issues to make informed decisions about where to place their capital.

Chapter 7: AI and Cybersecurity: The Need for Robust Protection

As artificial intelligence becomes more deeply integrated into various industries and everyday technologies, the rising threat of cyberattacks on AI systems has emerged as a critical concern. AI, by its very nature, relies on vast amounts of data and complex algorithms, making it an attractive target for hackers seeking to exploit vulnerabilities in these systems. The growing dependence on AI in sensitive sectors such as healthcare, finance, and critical infrastructure has further heightened the stakes, as successful cyberattacks on AI systems could lead to widespread disruption, financial losses, and even physical harm.

One of the primary threats AI systems face is **data manipulation**. AI algorithms depend heavily on the integrity of the data they are trained on and use to make decisions. If an attacker can gain access to an AI system and alter the data—whether by injecting malicious data or corrupting existing datasets—the AI's outputs and decisions can be compromised. This type of attack, known as data poisoning, could have serious consequences. For example, in healthcare, compromised AI systems could misdiagnose diseases or suggest incorrect treatment plans. In finance, AI algorithms could be tricked into making poor investment decisions or approving fraudulent transactions, leading to significant losses.

Another concern is the potential for **model theft**, where attackers steal proprietary AI models or intellectual property. AI models often require significant resources and expertise to develop, and if stolen, they can be replicated or altered by competitors or malicious actors. This not only represents a financial loss for the company but can also compromise the security and privacy of users if the stolen model is used for malicious purposes. For instance, AI models used in facial recognition or biometric authentication could be exploited to bypass security systems or commit identity theft.

Moreover, the **adversarial attacks** on AI systems present a unique challenge. In an adversarial attack, small, carefully crafted changes are made to the input data, which cause the AI system to make incorrect decisions. For example, a slight modification to an image of a stop sign could cause an AI-powered autonomous vehicle to misinterpret the sign and fail to stop, leading to potential accidents. These attacks are particularly concerning because they exploit the AI system's reliance on precise data patterns, and even small changes can lead to catastrophic outcomes.

Given these threats, investors are becoming increasingly aware of the importance of strong **cybersecurity measures** in AI companies. Identifying companies that prioritize cybersecurity can help investors mitigate risks and protect their investments. Here are a few key indicators that investors can look for when evaluating the cybersecurity posture of AI companies:

1. **Commitment to Security by Design**: One of the first things investors should look for is whether a company integrates cybersecurity into the design of its AI systems from the very beginning. This "security by design" approach ensures that AI models and algorithms are built with security in mind, rather than as an afterthought. Companies that follow this approach typically conduct thorough risk assessments during the development phase and implement safeguards such as encryption, authentication protocols, and secure data handling practices. Investors should prioritize companies that emphasize security at every stage of AI development.

2. **Regular Audits and Vulnerability Assessments**: AI companies that take cybersecurity seriously often conduct regular security audits and vulnerability assessments. These assessments help identify weaknesses in AI systems and ensure that they are addressed before attackers can exploit them. Investors

should look for companies that not only perform these audits but also publicize their results or demonstrate transparency in how they handle security risks. Companies that proactively seek out potential vulnerabilities and engage third-party experts for security assessments are generally more trustworthy.

3. **Robust Data Protection Practices**: Since AI systems rely heavily on data, protecting this data is paramount. Investors should evaluate how AI companies manage data privacy and security. Look for companies that use encryption techniques to protect data both at rest and in transit, ensuring that even if data is intercepted, it cannot be easily accessed or manipulated. Additionally, companies that adopt strong data governance policies—such as limiting access to sensitive data, anonymizing user data, and complying with data protection regulations like GDPR—demonstrate a higher level of responsibility in managing data.

4. **Adoption of Advanced Cybersecurity Tools**: Companies that invest in state-of-the-art cybersecurity tools are more likely to be resilient against cyberattacks. These tools include firewalls, intrusion detection systems (IDS), and endpoint security solutions designed to monitor and prevent unauthorized access. AI companies should also be employing machine learning and AI-driven cybersecurity solutions themselves, as these can detect and respond to threats in real-time, adapting to new attack vectors more effectively than traditional security tools. Investors should inquire about the specific tools and technologies that AI companies use to safeguard their systems.
5. **Incident Response Plans**: A strong indicator of a company's cybersecurity readiness is the presence of a comprehensive incident response plan. Even the most secure systems are not immune to attacks, and companies must be prepared to respond quickly and effectively if a breach occurs. Investors should look for AI

companies that have clear, well-documented incident response protocols, which include steps for identifying, containing, and mitigating cyberattacks. Companies that frequently test and update their incident response plans are better positioned to minimize the impact of potential breaches.

6. **Track Record of Security and Compliance**: Investors can also evaluate a company's cybersecurity strength by examining its track record. Companies that have a history of protecting their systems from breaches and that have demonstrated compliance with relevant security standards are often safer bets. Look for companies that adhere to industry-specific security standards, such as ISO/IEC 27001 for information security management, or that have achieved certifications from recognized cybersecurity organizations. A strong compliance history and a commitment to industry best practices signal that the company takes its security obligations seriously.

7. **Collaboration with Cybersecurity Experts**: Many AI companies collaborate with external cybersecurity firms or researchers to strengthen their security posture. Companies that engage with white-hat hackers, participate in bug bounty programs, or collaborate with academic institutions on security research are actively working to identify and address vulnerabilities. This level of collaboration often reflects a commitment to staying ahead of emerging threats and reinforces trust in the company's ability to defend its AI systems against cyberattacks.

In summary, the rising threat of cyberattacks on AI systems presents a significant risk to both AI companies and their investors. However, by focusing on companies that prioritize strong cybersecurity measures, investors can mitigate some of these risks. Key factors to look for include a commitment to security by design, regular audits, robust data protection practices, advanced security tools, a solid incident response plan, and a proven track record of compliance. By carefully evaluating these elements, investors can identify companies that are better positioned to defend against cyberattacks and continue to thrive in an increasingly digital and connected world.

As artificial intelligence becomes more integral to modern industries and everyday technologies, the importance of cybersecurity in safeguarding AI advancements cannot be overstated. AI systems, by their very nature, process vast amounts of data and perform tasks that are critical to the operations of businesses, governments, and even personal devices. With this increased reliance on AI comes the heightened risk of cyberattacks that could compromise these systems, leading to potentially catastrophic consequences.

One of the most critical reasons cybersecurity is so essential for AI is the protection of data. AI systems depend on large datasets to function effectively, whether for training machine learning models, making real-time decisions, or providing insights that drive business processes. Without robust cybersecurity, this data is vulnerable to attacks, manipulation, or theft. If the integrity of an AI system's data is compromised, the system may produce inaccurate results or make flawed decisions, which could have severe ramifications. For example, in healthcare, an AI model used for diagnosing diseases could be rendered ineffective if its data were corrupted, leading to misdiagnoses and poor patient outcomes. In finance, compromised AI systems could approve fraudulent transactions, resulting in financial loss and a breach of trust with customers.

In addition to data protection, cybersecurity is crucial in preventing malicious actors from manipulating AI models directly. Hackers could potentially interfere with the algorithms that underpin AI systems, causing them to behave in unpredictable or harmful ways. Known as adversarial attacks, these attempts involve subtly altering input data so that the AI system misinterprets it. For example, by slightly modifying an image or signal, an attacker could trick an AI-driven autonomous vehicle into misreading a traffic sign, posing a threat to passenger safety. The ability to guard against such vulnerabilities is a key aspect of ensuring the safe and reliable deployment of AI technologies.

The risk of cyberattacks on AI systems extends beyond just individual users or companies. As AI becomes more deeply embedded in critical infrastructure—such as energy grids, transportation networks, and defense systems—the consequences of a breach could be far-reaching. For instance, an attack on AI systems managing energy distribution could cause widespread power outages, while interference in AI-driven defense systems could lead to national security risks. In these contexts, the failure to secure AI systems effectively could have disastrous consequences on a national or even global scale.

Another important aspect of cybersecurity in AI is maintaining the intellectual property and proprietary technologies that companies have invested heavily in developing. AI models and algorithms often represent significant time, effort, and resources. If a competitor or malicious actor manages to steal these models, not only does it threaten the company's competitive advantage, but it also compromises the security and privacy of the data used to train these systems. In a landscape where companies compete to develop the most advanced AI solutions, safeguarding intellectual property is just as crucial as protecting the data and systems themselves.

Furthermore, as AI continues to evolve, new security threats are constantly emerging. The rapid pace of AI development means that cybersecurity measures must also keep up with these changes. Companies that develop AI must not only protect their current systems but also anticipate future threats, such as the use of AI by cybercriminals to launch more sophisticated attacks. This calls for an ongoing commitment to cybersecurity research and innovation to ensure that as AI becomes more advanced, so too do the protections that guard it.

Finally, the importance of cybersecurity in AI extends to building public trust in these technologies. As AI becomes more integrated into everyday life, people must feel confident that the systems they rely on—whether for online shopping, banking, or healthcare—are secure from breaches and attacks. A well-secured AI system fosters trust and encourages widespread adoption, while high-profile security breaches could erode public confidence and slow the advancement of AI technologies.

In conclusion, cybersecurity is critical in ensuring the safe and effective advancement of AI. It protects the data that powers AI systems, safeguards against manipulation and adversarial attacks, and maintains the intellectual property that drives innovation. Moreover, it ensures that AI systems embedded in critical infrastructure remain secure, preventing potentially catastrophic consequences. As AI continues to shape the future of industries and societies, the role of cybersecurity in protecting these systems will only become more important, making it a cornerstone of responsible AI development.

Chapter 8: Separating Hype from Reality

The rapid growth and transformative potential of artificial intelligence have led to significant excitement and optimism around AI companies. However, with this excitement comes the risk of overhyping AI technologies and companies, often leading to inflated valuations and exaggerated claims about the capabilities of AI products and services. In such an environment, investors must be vigilant about identifying potential fraud and recognizing when companies are making claims that may not be grounded in reality. Understanding how to spot these warning signs and conducting thorough due diligence are key to making informed investment decisions in the AI space.

One of the dangers of overhyping AI companies is that it can lead to unrealistic expectations. Startups and established companies alike may overstate the capabilities of their AI models or promise breakthroughs that are not yet achievable. This can attract significant investment, but when the technology fails to live up to the hype, stock prices can crash, resulting in substantial financial losses for investors. In some cases, companies may claim to be further along in AI development than they actually are, either to attract investors or to position themselves as leaders in a competitive market. These exaggerated claims can distort the market and lead to unsustainable growth, setting the stage for a collapse when the true limitations of the technology are revealed.

One way to identify potential fraud or exaggerated claims is by closely examining the **transparency** of a company's AI technology. Companies that are genuinely making progress in AI development are often willing to share details about how their models work, the data they use, and the specific challenges they are addressing. On the other hand, companies that offer vague descriptions of their technology or rely heavily on buzzwords without explaining the underlying mechanisms may be trying to conceal the true state of their AI capabilities. Investors should be wary of companies that overemphasize the potential of their AI solutions without providing concrete evidence or technical details to back up their claims.

Another red flag to watch for is **overstated timelines** for delivering AI breakthroughs. Developing and deploying advanced AI technologies often takes years of research, testing, and iteration. Companies that promise rapid implementation of cutting-edge AI solutions may be underestimating the challenges involved or deliberately overhyping their progress. Unrealistically short timelines for delivering AI products or services should be a signal for investors to dig deeper into the company's claims and assess whether they are grounded in feasible technology development cycles.

The role of **due diligence** becomes critical when evaluating AI companies to avoid falling victim to overhyped claims or fraudulent activity. Due diligence involves a thorough investigation into the financial health, technological expertise, and business practices of a company to assess whether it is a viable investment. One of the first steps in due diligence is examining a company's **financial health**. Investors should review financial statements, including balance sheets, income statements, and cash flow reports, to understand the company's revenue streams, profitability, and overall stability. Companies that are burning through cash without clear paths to profitability may be relying on hype to sustain themselves, making them risky investments.

In addition to financial health, investors must evaluate a company's **technological expertise**. This involves assessing the credentials of the team leading AI development, including their experience and track record in the field. Companies with strong leadership teams that have demonstrated success in AI or related technologies are more likely to have the expertise needed to develop viable AI products. Investors should also look at the **patents** or intellectual property the company holds, as these can be indicators of genuine innovation and technological progress. Furthermore, investors should seek out third-party validation of the company's technology, such as peer-reviewed research, collaborations with reputable academic institutions, or endorsements from industry experts.

Another aspect of due diligence involves evaluating the **competitive landscape** in which the AI company operates. A company that is overly secretive about its competitors or fails to acknowledge the challenges posed by established players in the field may be trying to create an illusion of dominance where none exists. By understanding how the company's AI technology compares to that of its competitors, investors can get a clearer picture of its strengths and weaknesses, as well as its potential for long-term success.

Investors should also look for companies that have a **track record of delivering on promises**. This can be assessed by reviewing the company's history of product launches, partnerships, and milestones. Companies that have consistently met development goals and successfully brought AI solutions to market are generally more reliable than those with a history of delays or unmet expectations. This track record is particularly important when evaluating startups or younger AI companies, as it offers insight into their ability to execute on ambitious plans.

Another important element of due diligence is assessing the **ethics and transparency** of a company's AI practices. Companies that are committed to ethical AI development often take steps to ensure their algorithms are free from bias, their data handling practices are secure, and their AI models are transparent and explainable. Investors should look for companies that are proactive in addressing ethical concerns and are willing to engage with regulators, industry experts, and the public about how their AI technologies are being developed and used. Companies that avoid or downplay discussions about the ethical implications of their AI systems may be more likely to face regulatory or reputational risks in the future.

In conclusion, the dangers of overhyping AI companies are real and can lead to significant financial losses if investors do not exercise caution. By paying attention to red flags such as vague technology descriptions, unrealistic timelines, and lack of transparency, investors can protect themselves from falling victim to exaggerated claims. Conducting thorough due diligence—focusing on a company's financial health, technological expertise, competitive position, and ethical practices—will help investors make informed decisions and avoid the risks associated with overhyped AI ventures. In a fast-evolving and competitive market like AI, these steps are essential for identifying companies that have the potential for real innovation and long-term success.

When analyzing AI investment opportunities, it is essential to consider several key factors that will help you identify companies with strong growth potential and long-term sustainability. AI is a rapidly evolving field, and not all companies will succeed in turning their innovations into profitable ventures. By focusing on these critical elements, investors can make informed decisions and minimize the risks associated with AI investments.

One of the most important factors to consider is the **quality of the leadership team**. The people behind a company are often the most significant determinant of its success. In AI, where technological innovation and strategic decision-making are paramount, having a leadership team with a strong track record in AI research and development is crucial. Look for executives and founders with expertise in AI, machine learning, data science, and technology development. Companies that have leaders who have successfully brought AI products to market or who have previous experience at reputable tech companies are more likely to navigate the complex challenges that come with AI development.

Another key factor is the company's **intellectual property (IP)**. AI companies that hold valuable patents or have developed proprietary algorithms and models are more likely to have a competitive advantage in the marketplace. Patents provide legal protection against competitors, and proprietary technology can be a major differentiator in a crowded field. Companies that continually invest in research and development to expand their IP portfolio are often better positioned for long-term growth. Investors should also assess how well the company's IP aligns with emerging trends in AI, such as advancements in natural language processing, computer vision, or autonomous systems.

Market relevance is also a critical consideration. AI companies should be targeting industries and applications where AI can have a transformative impact. Sectors such as healthcare, finance, automotive, and manufacturing are seeing significant AI adoption due to the technology's ability to optimize processes, reduce costs, and create new value. When evaluating an AI company, consider how well its products or services align with the needs of these industries and whether its solutions offer a clear value proposition. Companies that are solving real-world problems with their AI technologies, rather than just developing AI for the sake of it, are more likely to gain market traction and secure long-term customers.

The company's **business model** and revenue streams are equally important when assessing AI investment opportunities. Some AI companies may offer software-as-a-service (SaaS) models, where customers subscribe to use the company's AI-powered tools, while others may provide AI consulting services or sell AI-enabled hardware. It's essential to understand how the company plans to generate consistent revenue and whether its business model is scalable. Look for companies that have diversified revenue streams and a clear path to profitability, especially if they are still in the early stages of development.

Investors should also consider the company's **technological infrastructure**. AI companies require significant computational resources to develop and run their models, particularly for deep learning and other advanced machine learning techniques. Companies that invest in powerful hardware, cloud computing platforms, and data storage solutions are better equipped to handle the demands of AI development. Additionally, companies that partner with established cloud providers, such as Amazon Web Services (AWS), Google Cloud, or Microsoft Azure, often have access to scalable and reliable infrastructure, which can be a significant advantage.

The **quality and quantity of data** a company has access to is another crucial factor in AI investments. AI models rely on vast datasets to learn, improve, and make accurate predictions. Companies that have access to unique or proprietary datasets—whether from customer interactions, sensors, or partnerships—are better positioned to train and refine their AI systems. Additionally, companies that prioritize data quality, ensuring that the data is clean, unbiased, and relevant, are more likely to develop robust AI models. In contrast, companies with limited or poor-quality data may struggle to deliver accurate and reliable AI solutions.

The company's ability to **adapt to regulatory and ethical concerns** is becoming increasingly important in the AI landscape. As AI technologies are integrated into critical areas like healthcare, finance, and law enforcement, regulatory oversight is expected to increase. Companies that demonstrate a commitment to ethical AI practices, including transparency, data privacy, and fairness, are more likely to avoid regulatory hurdles and build trust with customers and investors. Investors should look for companies that have established clear policies for data usage, algorithmic fairness, and compliance with regulations such as the European Union's General Data Protection Regulation (GDPR) or other relevant laws.

Strategic partnerships can also be an indicator of a company's potential success. AI companies that collaborate with established players in the tech, healthcare, finance, or automotive industries often gain access to valuable resources, including expertise, data, and distribution channels. These partnerships can accelerate product development and market entry, giving AI companies a competitive edge. Furthermore, partnerships with universities and research institutions can help companies stay at the forefront of AI innovation by incorporating the latest advancements from academia into their products and services.

Customer base and adoption rate are also key metrics to evaluate. A growing customer base and high adoption rates indicate that a company's AI solutions are resonating with the market. Investors should examine the company's customer retention rates and whether it has secured long-term contracts with major clients. A solid customer base not only provides a stable revenue stream but also demonstrates that the company's AI solutions are delivering tangible value. Startups with a strong track record of securing partnerships with large enterprises or government agencies often have a greater chance of success.

Finally, consider the company's **ability to scale**. AI companies with scalable technologies and business models are more likely to achieve significant growth as demand for AI continues to rise. Investors should assess whether the company's technology can be adapted to new markets or industries and whether its infrastructure can handle a growing number of users or clients. Companies with a flexible, adaptable approach to AI development are better equipped to scale and capitalize on emerging opportunities in the global AI market.

In summary, when analyzing AI investment opportunities, it's crucial to focus on factors such as the leadership team's expertise, the company's intellectual property and patents, market relevance, and the strength of its business model. Additionally, a company's technological infrastructure, data quality, ethical considerations, and ability to form strategic partnerships play significant roles in its potential for success. By carefully evaluating these factors, investors can identify AI companies that are well-positioned for growth and long-term profitability in a competitive and rapidly evolving industry.

Chapter 9: AI Investment Opportunities in Startups

Venture capital has long been a driving force behind the growth of emerging technologies, and the artificial intelligence sector is no exception. Venture capitalists (VCs) are drawn to AI startups because of their potential to revolutionize entire industries with innovative and disruptive solutions. However, investing in AI startups is a high-risk, high-reward strategy that requires both deep industry knowledge and an appetite for uncertainty. For investors who are willing to take on the risk, the rewards can be substantial, as successful AI startups have the potential to scale rapidly and generate exponential returns.

The high-risk nature of investing in AI startups stems from several factors. First, the **early-stage nature** of many AI companies means that they are often unproven in terms of their technology, market fit, or revenue generation. These startups are typically still in the development phase, with products that may be years away from reaching commercial viability. As a result, many AI startups face significant challenges in terms of funding, product development, and market adoption. Additionally, the rapid pace of innovation in AI means that what is cutting-edge today may quickly become obsolete, leaving startups vulnerable to being outpaced by competitors or new technological advancements.

Despite these risks, the **potential rewards** of investing in AI startups are substantial. AI technologies have the power to disrupt traditional industries by solving problems in ways that were previously unimaginable. For example, AI startups are developing solutions that can optimize supply chains, automate customer service, enhance cybersecurity, improve healthcare outcomes, and even revolutionize autonomous transportation. The ability of AI to analyze vast amounts of data and make real-time decisions is opening up new opportunities for startups to address inefficiencies, reduce costs, and create value for businesses and consumers alike.

Startups are particularly well-suited to **disrupt traditional industries** because they are often more agile and innovative than larger, established companies. Free from the constraints of legacy systems or bureaucratic processes, AI startups can move quickly to bring new products to market, iterate on their technology, and respond to customer feedback. This agility allows them to experiment with cutting-edge AI technologies, such as deep learning, natural language processing, and computer vision, and apply them in ways that solve specific, industry-wide problems.

In the healthcare industry, for example, AI startups are using machine learning algorithms to develop diagnostic tools that can detect diseases earlier and more accurately than traditional methods. Startups like **PathAI** are working on AI-powered tools that assist pathologists in diagnosing cancer by analyzing medical images at a scale and precision that is beyond human capabilities. These innovations are disrupting the traditional approach to medical diagnostics and could dramatically improve patient outcomes by enabling faster and more accurate treatments. The promise of AI in healthcare is vast, with startups also focusing on areas like drug discovery, personalized medicine, and patient monitoring.

In the **finance sector**, AI startups are reshaping the way financial institutions manage risk, detect fraud, and engage with customers. Companies like **Kensho Technologies** have developed AI systems that analyze vast amounts of financial data to provide insights into market trends, geopolitical events, and economic conditions. These tools are helping financial professionals make more informed decisions, while AI-powered algorithms are being used in high-frequency trading, credit scoring, and loan approvals. Startups are disrupting traditional financial services by offering more efficient, accurate, and scalable solutions, often at a fraction of the cost of legacy systems.

The **retail and e-commerce** sectors are also being transformed by AI startups that are using machine learning and predictive analytics to enhance customer experiences and optimize operations. Startups like **Zebra Medical Vision** have developed AI algorithms that help retailers better understand customer behavior and preferences, enabling more personalized recommendations, targeted advertising, and efficient inventory management. These innovations are enabling retailers to compete in an increasingly digital marketplace by providing a level of customization and efficiency that was previously unattainable.

In **transportation**, AI startups are at the forefront of developing autonomous vehicles, which have the potential to disrupt not only the automotive industry but also logistics, delivery services, and urban transportation. Companies like **Aurora**

Innovation are developing AI-driven self-driving technology that could reduce the need for human drivers, lower transportation costs, and make roads safer. These startups are challenging traditional automotive manufacturers by offering a vision of the future where AI-powered vehicles are more efficient, safer, and environmentally friendly. The potential impact of autonomous vehicles extends far beyond just cars, with startups exploring AI solutions for trucks, drones, and other forms of transportation.

The **manufacturing industry** is another area where AI startups are making significant inroads. Startups focused on robotics and automation, such as **UiPath**, are developing AI-driven systems that can automate repetitive tasks, reduce human error, and increase production efficiency. By integrating AI with industrial robots, these startups are enabling manufacturers to optimize their supply chains, reduce costs, and improve product quality. This is leading to a shift in the traditional manufacturing model, where AI and robotics are increasingly becoming central to production processes.

In addition to disrupting traditional industries, AI startups are also creating entirely new markets and business models. The rise of **AI-as-a-Service (AIaaS)** has allowed companies of all sizes to access advanced AI tools and platforms without the need for significant upfront investment in infrastructure or expertise. Startups like **C3.ai** provide cloud-based AI solutions that businesses can use to integrate machine learning, predictive analytics, and automation into their operations. By offering AI solutions on a subscription basis, these startups are democratizing access to AI technology and enabling companies across industries to leverage the power of AI.

For investors, the high-reward potential of AI startups comes from the fact that these companies are often at the cutting edge of technology and have the ability to scale rapidly. Once an AI startup successfully develops a product that gains market traction, it can experience exponential growth as it attracts customers, expands into new markets, and secures additional funding. The scalable nature of AI solutions means that once the technology is developed, it can be applied across multiple industries and geographies, generating significant revenue streams.

However, investing in AI startups requires careful due diligence and an understanding of the **unique challenges** these companies face. Investors should assess the quality of the startup's leadership team, the scalability of its technology, and the strength of its intellectual property. Additionally, understanding the competitive landscape and the startup's ability to execute on its vision is critical for making informed investment decisions.

Venture capital and AI startups represent a high-risk, high-reward investment strategy. Startups are disrupting traditional industries with innovative AI solutions, from healthcare and finance to retail and transportation. While the risks are significant, the potential for exponential growth makes AI startups an attractive opportunity for investors who are willing to take on uncertainty and support the next generation of technological innovation. By carefully analyzing the strengths and weaknesses of AI startups, investors can position themselves to benefit from the transformative impact of AI on global industries.

Several AI startups have achieved remarkable success by leveraging innovative technologies to disrupt traditional industries and deliver rapid growth. These companies have developed cutting-edge solutions that address complex challenges in sectors such as healthcare, finance, and logistics, demonstrating the transformative power of AI in real-world applications. Here are a few notable examples of AI startups that have achieved significant growth through their innovative use of artificial intelligence.

One of the most well-known examples is **UiPath**, a startup that has become a leader in robotic process automation (RPA) by integrating AI into its software solutions. UiPath uses AI to automate repetitive tasks within businesses, such as data entry, invoicing, and customer support. By employing machine learning algorithms, UiPath's platform learns from human actions to perform these tasks faster and with fewer errors than manual processes. The company's software has been adopted by major enterprises across various industries, including banking, healthcare, and telecommunications, where it helps organizations save time and reduce costs by automating workflows. UiPath's rapid growth led to a successful initial public offering (IPO) in 2021, with the company achieving a multibillion-dollar valuation, making it one of the most successful AI startups to date.

In the healthcare sector, **PathAI** is an AI-driven startup that has revolutionized medical diagnostics through machine learning. The company uses AI algorithms to analyze medical images, particularly in pathology, to assist doctors in diagnosing diseases such as cancer. PathAI's platform can process and interpret tissue samples at a much higher speed and accuracy than traditional methods, reducing the chances of misdiagnosis and improving patient outcomes. By partnering with pharmaceutical companies, hospitals, and research institutions, PathAI has gained significant traction in the healthcare industry, accelerating its growth. The company's ability to use AI to solve critical challenges in diagnostics has led to significant investments and made it a key player in the rapidly evolving field of AI in healthcare.

Another AI startup that has seen rapid growth is **Zebra Medical Vision**, which focuses on applying AI to medical imaging. The company's AI-powered platform is designed to detect a wide range of medical conditions by analyzing medical scans such as X-rays, MRIs, and CT scans. Zebra

Medical Vision's algorithms can identify early signs of diseases like cancer, cardiovascular conditions, and liver disease, often before symptoms appear. This capability has allowed healthcare providers to improve early detection rates and offer more effective treatments. The startup's AI-driven approach to medical imaging has garnered partnerships with major healthcare providers around the world, contributing to its rapid expansion. Zebra Medical Vision's success in the healthcare industry highlights the potential of AI to revolutionize diagnostics and treatment.

In the financial sector, **Kensho Technologies** is an AI startup that has gained prominence by developing AI-driven solutions for financial analysis and decision-making. Kensho's platform uses natural language processing and machine learning to analyze vast amounts of data, including financial reports, news articles, and economic indicators. The company's AI tools provide insights into market trends, geopolitical events, and investment opportunities, helping financial professionals make more informed decisions. Kensho's technology has been adopted by some of the world's largest financial institutions, including Goldman Sachs and S&P Global, where it is used to streamline research and analysis processes. Kensho's innovative use of AI to enhance financial decision-making has propelled the company to rapid growth, culminating in its acquisition by S&P Global for $550 million, making it one of the largest AI acquisitions in the financial sector.

C3.ai is another example of an AI startup that has achieved rapid growth by offering AI-as-a-Service (AIaaS) solutions to enterprises across multiple industries. The company's platform allows businesses to deploy AI applications for predictive analytics, supply chain optimization, and customer engagement without needing to invest in the infrastructure required to build these systems from scratch. By offering AI tools that are easy to integrate and scale, C3.ai has attracted a wide range of clients, including companies in the energy, manufacturing, and healthcare sectors. The flexibility and scalability of C3.ai's platform have driven its rapid expansion, and the company went public in 2020, raising $651 million in its IPO. C3.ai's success showcases the growing demand for AI-powered solutions that can be easily deployed across industries to drive operational efficiency and innovation.

In the transportation and logistics space, **Nuro** has emerged as a key player in the development of autonomous delivery vehicles. Nuro's AI-powered self-driving vehicles are designed to deliver goods such as groceries, meals, and parcels directly to consumers' doorsteps. By using AI to navigate urban environments safely and efficiently, Nuro's vehicles eliminate the need for human drivers, reducing delivery costs and making last-mile logistics more efficient. The startup has formed partnerships with major retailers such as Kroger and Domino's Pizza, accelerating its growth and expanding its operations across multiple U.S. cities. Nuro's innovative use of AI in autonomous delivery has positioned it as a leader in the emerging field of AI-driven logistics, with the company raising over $1 billion in funding to fuel its expansion.

Another example of an AI startup achieving rapid growth is **Scale AI**, which specializes in providing data labeling services for companies developing AI models. Scale AI's platform uses machine learning to automate the process of annotating large datasets, which is a critical step in training AI models. The company's clients include some of the biggest names in tech, including Google, Uber, and OpenAI, who rely on Scale AI's platform to efficiently prepare their data for machine learning applications. The growing demand for high-quality data to train AI models has driven Scale AI's rapid growth, and the company has become a key enabler of AI development across industries. Scale AI's success underscores the importance of data preparation in the AI ecosystem and highlights the potential for startups that provide essential infrastructure for AI development.

These real-world examples demonstrate the ability of AI startups to achieve rapid growth by addressing specific challenges and creating innovative solutions in a wide range of industries. Whether through automating business processes, enhancing healthcare diagnostics, improving financial decision-making, or revolutionizing logistics, AI startups are disrupting traditional industries and creating new opportunities for growth. The success of these companies highlights the transformative potential of AI and the significant rewards that can come from investing in startups at the forefront of this technological revolution.

Chapter 10: Long-Term AI Investment Strategies

Staying informed about the latest advancements and trends in artificial intelligence is crucial for anyone involved in AI investing. AI is a rapidly evolving field, with new technologies, applications, and breakthroughs emerging regularly. For investors, maintaining an up-to-date understanding of these developments is essential to making informed decisions, identifying promising opportunities, and mitigating risks. AI's fast pace of change means that today's cutting-edge innovation could become tomorrow's industry standard—or be replaced by something even more advanced. Therefore, continuous learning is not just beneficial but necessary to navigate this dynamic space.

One of the best ways to stay informed about AI advancements is by attending **conferences and industry events**. These gatherings provide an opportunity to hear directly from thought leaders, researchers, and industry professionals who are at the forefront of AI development. Conferences like NeurIPS (Conference on Neural Information Processing Systems), the AI Summit, and the MIT AI and Machine Learning Conference are among the premier events where cutting-edge research and applications are showcased. By attending these events, investors can gain valuable insights into emerging technologies, network with innovators, and better understand the direction in which AI is heading. Furthermore, these events often feature presentations from AI startups and established companies, giving investors a firsthand look at new products and services that could shape the market.

In addition to conferences, subscribing to **industry reports** is another essential tool for staying informed about AI trends. Many consulting firms, such as McKinsey, Deloitte, and PwC, regularly publish detailed reports on AI and its impact on various industries. These reports analyze current trends, predict future developments, and provide insights into how AI is being adopted across sectors like healthcare, finance, automotive, and retail. Investors can use these reports to identify which industries are experiencing the most rapid AI growth and which companies are leading the charge. For example, McKinsey's "Global AI Survey" offers a comprehensive overview of AI adoption, highlighting key applications, challenges, and investment areas. Reading such reports ensures that investors are well-versed in both the opportunities and risks associated with AI investment.

Expert analysis from leading AI researchers, venture capitalists, and industry veterans is another valuable source of information. Following blogs, podcasts, and social media accounts from AI experts can provide timely updates on the latest advancements, challenges, and debates in the AI space. Prominent figures like Andrew Ng, Fei-Fei Li, and Kai-Fu Lee often share their insights on platforms like Medium, Twitter, and LinkedIn, where they discuss trends such as machine learning models, ethical concerns, and AI's societal impact. By engaging with expert analysis, investors can deepen their understanding of the technical, ethical, and market dynamics shaping AI. Additionally, investors can explore research papers from major AI research labs like OpenAI, DeepMind, and Google AI to keep track of groundbreaking developments in the field.

Subscribing to **newsletters and publications** focused on AI and technology is another effective way to stay current. Outlets such as MIT Technology Review, Wired, and AI Trends regularly cover the latest advancements in AI, including interviews with industry leaders, updates on regulations, and new applications of AI in different sectors. These publications offer digestible, regular updates that can help investors stay on top of emerging trends, from new AI models and algorithms to government policies impacting AI development.

For investors, **continuous learning** is especially important because the AI landscape is not static. New technologies, regulatory frameworks, and market dynamics can quickly change the investment landscape. An investor who was well-versed in AI technologies five years ago may find that today's innovations, such as transformers, generative AI, or reinforcement learning, have dramatically altered the playing field. Staying informed allows investors to make timely decisions about their portfolios, whether that means seizing new opportunities or mitigating risks in the face of changing market conditions.

Attending **workshops and webinars** is another way to remain educated about AI advancements. Many organizations and educational platforms, such as Coursera, edX, and Udacity, offer AI-related courses that dive deep into specific topics like machine learning, natural language processing, or AI ethics. These courses can help investors not only understand the technical aspects of AI but also how these technologies are being applied in real-world scenarios. For example, a course on machine learning might explain how predictive algorithms are transforming industries like healthcare and finance. By engaging with these educational resources, investors can develop a more nuanced understanding of the technology they are investing in, leading to more informed investment decisions.

Networking with **industry professionals** is also key to staying ahead in the AI space. Engaging with AI researchers, engineers, and other investors through industry forums, LinkedIn groups, or AI-focused meetups can provide valuable insights into emerging technologies and market trends. Building a network of AI professionals allows investors to exchange ideas, share knowledge, and gain a more comprehensive understanding of where AI is headed. Investors can also benefit from joining **AI investment groups** or working with **venture capital firms** that specialize in technology investments. These groups often have access to proprietary information, exclusive reports, and early-stage investment opportunities, which can provide a competitive advantage in the fast-moving AI market.

It's also crucial for investors to stay informed about **AI regulations and ethical issues**, as these can significantly impact the investment landscape. Governments worldwide are grappling with how to regulate AI technologies, particularly in areas like data privacy, algorithmic bias, and the use of AI in surveillance. Regulations can affect AI companies' operations, especially those that rely on data-intensive processes, making it essential for investors to monitor regulatory developments. Investors should regularly review updates from regulatory bodies such as the European Union, which has taken a leading role in AI regulation with initiatives like the AI Act. Understanding how these regulations evolve will help investors anticipate potential challenges or opportunities that may arise due to changing legal frameworks.

Continuous learning is essential for AI investors who want to stay informed and make sound investment decisions. By attending conferences, subscribing to industry reports, following expert analysis, engaging with educational resources, and networking with professionals, investors can keep up with the latest advancements and trends in AI. In a field as fast-paced and transformative as AI, staying informed is not only a competitive advantage but also a necessity for long-term success. With AI technologies poised to reshape industries and societies, continuous learning will empower investors to identify the most promising opportunities and navigate the complexities of this rapidly evolving market.

Balancing short-term gains with long-term growth potential is one of the most important challenges for AI investors, as the field offers both immediate opportunities and long-term transformational possibilities. Navigating this balance effectively can help investors maximize returns while minimizing risks, but it requires a strategic approach that considers both the fast pace of AI innovation and the gradual development of certain AI-driven industries.

In the AI space, **short-term gains** often arise from rapid technological breakthroughs, successful product launches, or the adoption of AI technologies in specific industries. For instance, AI companies that introduce innovative products or services can experience significant stock price increases, especially if their technologies solve pressing problems in industries like healthcare, finance, or logistics. Investors who can identify companies on the verge of releasing a new AI-driven product or entering into a lucrative partnership may benefit from these short-term gains. Similarly, sectors like e-commerce, cybersecurity, and financial technology are witnessing rapid AI adoption, which has the potential to create near-term opportunities for investors as companies expand their use of AI to drive efficiencies and improve customer experiences.

However, focusing solely on short-term gains can lead to significant risks. AI companies often face **high volatility**, with stock prices rising and falling based on technological progress, market sentiment, or regulatory news. A product that seems revolutionary in the short term may not gain traction or could be overtaken by a competitor's superior technology. Therefore, while it's tempting to seek quick profits from the rapid adoption of AI in certain industries, investors must remain cautious and avoid overcommitting to companies based solely on short-term trends.

In contrast, **long-term growth potential** in AI lies in the transformative power of the technology across multiple industries over the coming decades. AI is expected to play a central role in sectors such as healthcare, autonomous transportation, manufacturing automation, and personalized medicine. These industries are still in the early stages of integrating AI, meaning it could take years or even decades for some of the most significant AI applications to fully materialize. Investors who focus on long-term growth potential are betting on the ability of AI companies to not only innovate but also scale their technologies, overcome regulatory challenges, and build sustainable business models.

A long-term approach requires patience, as some AI technologies will take time to achieve widespread adoption. For example, **autonomous vehicles** and **AI-driven drug discovery** are areas with enormous growth potential, but both face technical, regulatory, and ethical hurdles that may delay their widespread commercialization. However, investors who recognize the long-term potential of these technologies and are willing to hold their investments through the development and adoption phases could see substantial returns as AI becomes more deeply integrated into these industries.

One way to balance short-term gains with long-term growth potential is by **diversifying**

your AI investment portfolio. Rather than concentrating solely on early-stage AI startups or companies with high short-term volatility, investors can allocate their capital across a range of companies, from established tech giants like Google, Microsoft, and Nvidia, to smaller, emerging AI players. Established companies often provide a more stable foundation for long-term growth, as they have the resources, infrastructure, and customer base to scale AI innovations over time. Meanwhile, smaller AI startups might offer higher short-term rewards, especially if they achieve breakthrough successes or are acquired by larger companies. A diversified portfolio allows investors to benefit from the immediate upside of AI while maintaining exposure to companies that are well-positioned to capitalize on the future growth of AI-driven industries.

Rebalancing your portfolio periodically is another strategy to maintain the right balance between short-term gains and long-term growth. As

AI companies mature and their stock prices fluctuate, investors should periodically review their holdings to ensure that their portfolio aligns with their financial goals and risk tolerance. This might involve taking profits from short-term winners and reallocating funds to companies with stronger long-term growth prospects. Regular rebalancing allows investors to capture gains while still maintaining exposure to the AI trends that are expected to drive long-term value creation.

Another key to balancing short- and long-term potential is **staying informed about industry trends and company developments**. By continuously monitoring technological advancements, market dynamics, and regulatory changes, investors can adjust their strategies as necessary. For example, if a particular AI technology is gaining faster adoption than expected, investors might choose to increase their exposure to companies in that space. Conversely, if an AI-driven sector faces unforeseen challenges, such as regulatory setbacks or technical limitations, investors might reduce their holdings in that area to protect against downside risks.

Investors can also look for **AI companies with a clear roadmap** that balances both short- and long-term goals. Companies that have a pipeline of AI-driven products or services aimed at solving immediate industry challenges are more likely to deliver short-term gains, while those focused on foundational AI technologies with broad, long-term applications offer the potential for sustained growth. Companies that demonstrate a commitment to both near-term execution and long-term innovation are often better positioned to navigate the volatility of the AI market and generate returns over different time horizons.

For example, **Nvidia** is a company that has successfully balanced short-term gains with long-term growth potential. In the short term, Nvidia has benefited from the rapid adoption of its GPUs in AI applications, such as machine learning and deep learning, which have driven its stock price upward. At the same time, Nvidia is investing heavily in AI infrastructure for emerging fields like autonomous vehicles and AI-driven cloud computing, which are expected to fuel long-term growth. By developing a portfolio of products and solutions that address both immediate market needs and future opportunities, Nvidia offers a compelling case study of how companies can position themselves for success in both the short and long term.

In conclusion, balancing short-term gains with long-term growth potential requires a thoughtful, diversified approach to AI investment. While it's tempting to chase quick profits from the latest AI breakthroughs, investors must remain mindful of the risks and volatility associated with short-term plays. At the same time, focusing on long-term growth in industries where AI has the potential to transform entire sectors can lead to substantial returns, but only for those willing to be patient and navigate the challenges of emerging technologies. By diversifying investments, staying informed, and periodically rebalancing portfolios, investors can benefit from both the immediate and future opportunities that AI presents.

Chapter 11: The Future of AI

Artificial intelligence is playing an increasingly pivotal role in shaping the future of industries worldwide. Its evolving capabilities, fueled by advancements in machine learning, data analytics, and automation, are driving unprecedented transformations across sectors like healthcare, transportation, finance, and manufacturing. The technologies powered by AI are not only improving operational efficiencies but are also creating new business models, changing how companies engage with customers, and fundamentally altering how industries operate. As AI continues to mature, its role in shaping the future will only grow more pronounced, with emerging technologies like autonomous vehicles, healthcare diagnostics, and personalized AI services leading the charge.

One of the most exciting areas where AI is driving transformation is in **autonomous vehicles**. Self-driving cars are poised to disrupt not just the automotive industry but the broader transportation and logistics sectors. Companies like Tesla, Waymo, and Aurora Innovation are leveraging AI technologies such as computer vision, deep learning, and sensor fusion to develop autonomous driving systems that can navigate complex environments with minimal human intervention. These AI systems allow vehicles to analyze their surroundings in real time, making decisions on steering, braking, and acceleration with greater precision and speed than human drivers. The implications of this technology extend far beyond personal vehicles; autonomous trucks, delivery robots, and drones have the potential to revolutionize how goods are transported across cities and regions, reducing costs, improving safety, and enabling faster deliveries.

AI-powered autonomous vehicles also have the potential to reduce traffic accidents caused by human error, which remains a leading cause of fatalities on roads globally. By eliminating the human factor from driving, autonomous vehicles could make roads safer and more efficient, while also lowering emissions through optimized driving patterns and route planning. The ongoing development of autonomous vehicle technology is not without its challenges—regulatory hurdles, safety concerns, and technical limitations still need to be addressed. However, as these issues are resolved, autonomous vehicles will likely become a cornerstone of modern transportation, reshaping industries ranging from ride-sharing to freight logistics.

In the **healthcare sector**, AI is driving significant advancements in diagnostics and personalized medicine. Machine learning algorithms are now being used to analyze medical images, detect diseases, and predict patient outcomes with a level of accuracy that rivals or surpasses human doctors. AI-powered diagnostic tools, such as those developed by companies like PathAI and Zebra Medical Vision, can analyze large datasets of medical images (X-rays, MRIs, and CT scans) to detect subtle patterns and anomalies that might be missed by human eyes. These technologies are helping to identify conditions like cancer, heart disease, and neurological disorders earlier and more accurately, leading to better patient outcomes and more personalized treatment plans.

The role of AI in **personalized medicine** is particularly transformative. By analyzing vast amounts of patient data, including genetic information, medical history, and lifestyle factors, AI systems can predict how individual patients will respond to specific treatments. This level of personalization allows doctors to tailor treatments to the unique needs of each patient, improving effectiveness and reducing adverse side effects. AI-driven drug discovery is another area where the technology is making a major impact. Companies like Insilico Medicine are using AI to accelerate the discovery of new compounds, dramatically reducing the time and cost required to bring new drugs to market. This is revolutionizing the pharmaceutical industry and offering hope for more effective treatments for a wide range of diseases, including rare and complex conditions that have historically been difficult to treat.

As AI continues to evolve in healthcare, it is also enabling **remote patient monitoring** and telemedicine. AI-powered virtual health assistants can monitor patients' vital signs, detect changes in health conditions, and alert healthcare providers when intervention is needed. This capability is particularly valuable in managing chronic conditions like diabetes or heart disease, where continuous monitoring can help prevent complications and hospitalizations. Telemedicine platforms powered by AI are making healthcare more accessible, allowing patients to consult with doctors remotely and receive personalized care from the comfort of their homes. The integration of AI into healthcare is not only improving the accuracy and efficiency of medical care but is also reducing costs and making healthcare more equitable and accessible.

In addition to autonomous vehicles and healthcare diagnostics, AI is playing a major role in the rise of **personalized AI services** across various industries. Companies are increasingly using AI to provide hyper-personalized experiences to consumers, enhancing customer satisfaction and loyalty. In the retail and e-commerce sectors, AI-driven recommendation engines analyze customer behavior to offer personalized product suggestions, tailored marketing campaigns, and dynamic pricing strategies. Amazon, for instance, uses AI to recommend products based on a customer's past purchases, search history, and browsing patterns, creating a shopping experience that feels uniquely customized to each user.

AI is also transforming the world of **personal finance**. AI-powered financial advisors, often called robo-advisors, are helping consumers manage their investments, savings, and retirement plans with personalized strategies based on their financial goals, risk tolerance, and spending habits. These AI services, offered by companies like Betterment and Wealthfront, are democratizing access to sophisticated financial advice, making it available to a broader audience at a lower cost compared to traditional human advisors. In banking, AI is being used to enhance fraud detection, improve customer service through chatbots, and personalize loan offers based on real-time financial analysis.

Voice-activated AI assistants, such as Amazon's Alexa, Google Assistant, and Apple's Siri, are another example of personalized AI services that are becoming increasingly embedded in consumers' daily lives. These AI-powered assistants use natural language processing (NLP) to understand and respond to user commands, providing personalized assistance for tasks ranging from controlling smart home devices to managing schedules and answering questions. As voice recognition technology continues to improve, these AI assistants are expected to become even more integral to how people interact with technology, making daily life more convenient and efficient.

The future of **personalized AI services** goes beyond consumer applications. In the workplace, AI is being used to improve employee productivity and engagement by offering personalized learning and development programs. AI-driven platforms can analyze an employee's skills, performance data, and career goals to recommend specific training programs, career advancement opportunities, and personalized feedback. This kind of AI-driven personalization is transforming how companies manage talent and create a more engaged and productive workforce.

AI's evolving role in shaping future industries is already visible in the groundbreaking technologies emerging today, such as autonomous vehicles, AI-powered healthcare diagnostics, and personalized AI services. These innovations are not only improving efficiency and reducing costs but are also creating new business models and transforming customer experiences across various sectors. As AI technologies continue to mature, they will play an even greater role in defining the future of industries, driving innovation, and reshaping the global economy in profound ways.

The next wave of AI innovation is poised to have a profound impact on the global economy and investment landscape. As artificial intelligence matures, it is expected to reshape industries, drive unprecedented productivity gains, and create new markets, all while disrupting traditional business models. This transformation will present both opportunities and challenges for investors, as AI reshapes not only the competitive dynamics of existing industries but also the very nature of work, consumer behavior, and global economic growth.

One of the most significant ways AI will impact the global economy is through its ability to **boost productivity** across industries. AI-driven automation, machine learning, and data analytics are already helping companies optimize their operations, reduce costs, and increase efficiency. As AI technologies become more sophisticated, these benefits will be amplified, enabling companies to automate more complex tasks, analyze larger datasets, and make faster, data-driven decisions. For example, in manufacturing, AI-powered robots and predictive maintenance systems are reducing downtime, improving product quality, and lowering costs. In finance, AI algorithms are optimizing trading strategies, detecting fraud, and enhancing customer service through chatbots and robo-advisors. These productivity gains will contribute to overall economic growth, as businesses across sectors become more efficient and competitive.

However, the rise of AI also poses challenges for the **labor market**, as automation threatens to displace jobs in sectors such as manufacturing, retail, and customer service. AI systems are becoming increasingly capable of performing tasks traditionally handled by human workers, from data entry and customer support to driving and logistics management. While AI will undoubtedly create new jobs in areas such as AI development, data science, and AI-driven services, there will likely be significant disruptions to the workforce, particularly in lower-skilled jobs that are more susceptible to automation. For the global economy, this means that while AI-driven productivity gains could boost economic output, governments and businesses will need to address the social and economic implications of workforce displacement.

From an investment perspective, **AI's transformative impact** offers both risks and opportunities. Companies that successfully adopt and integrate AI technologies are likely to see significant growth, making them attractive investment opportunities. AI leaders in industries such as technology, healthcare, finance, and transportation will benefit from AI's ability to improve operational efficiencies, drive innovation, and open new revenue streams. For example, companies like Nvidia, Alphabet, and Microsoft, which are at the forefront of AI hardware and software development, are already reaping the rewards of AI's growth. Investors who identify companies that are leveraging AI to innovate and create new value will be well-positioned to capitalize on this trend.

However, AI's disruptive potential also introduces risks. Traditional companies that fail to adapt to AI-driven changes may find themselves outcompeted by more agile, AI-powered competitors. Industries such as retail, logistics, and transportation could experience significant disruption as AI technologies change the way businesses operate. For example, autonomous vehicles could disrupt the automotive and transportation industries, while AI-powered supply chain optimization could render traditional logistics models obsolete. Investors need to be mindful of these shifts and adjust their portfolios to reflect the industries and companies most likely to thrive in an AI-driven economy.

The next wave of AI innovation is also expected to **create entirely new markets and industries**, further reshaping the investment landscape. AI-driven technologies such as autonomous vehicles, smart cities, and AI-powered healthcare are still in their early stages, but they have the potential to generate trillions of dollars in new economic value. Autonomous vehicles alone could transform transportation, logistics, and urban planning, leading to the creation of new business models, such as autonomous ride-sharing services and AI-driven logistics companies. Similarly, smart cities powered by AI could revolutionize urban infrastructure, with AI systems optimizing energy usage, traffic flow, and public services. Investors who are able to identify early-stage opportunities in these emerging markets will have the potential to achieve substantial returns as these technologies mature.

In **healthcare**, AI is expected to drive major advancements in diagnostics, drug discovery, and personalized medicine. AI-powered diagnostics, such as those developed by companies like PathAI and Zebra Medical Vision, are already improving the accuracy and speed of disease detection. Meanwhile, AI is accelerating drug discovery by identifying new compounds and predicting how they will interact with biological systems, reducing the time and cost of bringing new drugs to market. The application of AI in healthcare is not only improving patient outcomes but also creating investment opportunities in AI-driven biotech startups and healthcare technology companies. As AI becomes more deeply integrated into the healthcare industry, investors can expect significant growth in AI-powered healthcare solutions and services.

Another area where AI is expected to have a major impact is **sustainability and climate change**. AI is being used to optimize energy consumption, reduce waste, and improve the efficiency of renewable energy sources such as solar and wind power. AI-powered systems can analyze vast amounts of data to predict energy demand, optimize grid management, and increase the efficiency of energy production and distribution. In agriculture, AI is being used to improve crop yields, reduce water usage, and minimize the use of pesticides, making farming more sustainable and environmentally friendly. As governments and businesses prioritize sustainability, AI will play a critical role in addressing climate change, creating new investment opportunities in green technology and sustainable industries.

AI is also expected to have a significant impact on **global trade and supply chains**. The COVID-19 pandemic exposed vulnerabilities in global supply chains, and businesses are now turning to AI to make their supply chains more resilient and efficient. AI-driven supply chain optimization tools can analyze data in real time to predict demand, manage inventory, and optimize shipping routes, reducing costs and improving efficiency. AI-powered automation is also being used in warehouses and manufacturing facilities to streamline production and reduce reliance on human labor. As businesses continue to globalize, AI will play an increasingly important role in managing complex, international supply chains, creating investment opportunities in AI-driven logistics and supply chain management companies.

Finally, the next wave of AI innovation will likely lead to **increased collaboration between humans and AI systems**. Rather than replacing humans entirely, AI is expected to augment human capabilities, enabling workers to be more productive and creative. In fields such as medicine, education, and creative industries, AI is already being used to assist professionals in performing their tasks more efficiently and effectively. For example, AI-powered tools can help doctors analyze medical data, teachers personalize learning experiences for students, and artists create new forms of digital art. This collaboration between humans and AI will create new opportunities for investment in AI tools that enhance human creativity and productivity.

In conclusion, the next wave of AI innovation will have a transformative impact on the global economy and investment landscape. AI-driven technologies will boost productivity, create new markets, and disrupt traditional industries, offering both opportunities and risks for investors. Companies that successfully adopt and integrate AI will thrive, while those that fail to adapt may struggle. Investors who stay informed about AI advancements, identify emerging markets, and recognize the potential of AI to reshape industries will be well-positioned to capitalize on the opportunities created by this technological revolution. As AI continues to evolve, its influence on the global economy will only grow, making it one of the most important forces shaping the future of investment.

Conclusion

In conclusion, artificial intelligence offers both tremendous opportunities and significant risks for investors. The rapid advancements in AI technologies are reshaping industries, driving new business models, and transforming the global economy in ways that present unique investment prospects. From autonomous vehicles and healthcare diagnostics to personalized AI services and smart cities, the potential for AI to revolutionize sectors is vast. However, the fast pace of change also introduces volatility and challenges, making it crucial for investors to balance short-term gains with long-term growth potential.

Key takeaways for AI investment include the importance of diversifying portfolios across established tech giants and emerging AI startups to spread risk while capturing innovation. Investors should stay informed about industry trends, regulatory changes, and technological developments by attending conferences, reading industry reports, and following expert analysis. Due diligence is critical when evaluating AI companies, particularly in assessing their leadership, intellectual property, scalability, and ethical practices.

AI's transformative potential is undeniable. It will reshape industries, create new markets, and redefine the way we live and work. Investors have a unique opportunity to not only profit from AI's growth but also to play a role in shaping the future by supporting companies that drive innovation and solve pressing global challenges. The next wave of AI will usher in new technologies that improve healthcare, enhance transportation, combat climate change, and elevate human creativity. Those who invest wisely in this space will help accelerate the adoption of these advancements and benefit from the economic value they create.

As AI continues to evolve, it is essential for investors to maintain a mindset of continuous learning. The AI landscape is dynamic, and staying ahead requires ongoing education and strategic decision-making. By remaining informed, embracing new ideas, and understanding both the opportunities and risks associated with AI, investors can position themselves for success in this rapidly changing world.

In closing, the future of AI is bright, and the potential for growth is immense. By carefully considering the key factors outlined in this book and making informed investment choices, readers can tap into AI's transformative power and contribute to shaping a better, more innovative future. Keep learning, stay curious, and make strategic investments to capitalize on the unprecedented opportunities that AI presents.

www.ingramcontent.com/pod-product-compliance
Lightning Source LLC
Chambersburg PA
CBHW052208220526

45471CB00004B/1862